Judging Women

A study of attitudes that rule our legal system

Polly Pattullo
Cartoons by Ros Asquith

NCCL Rights for Women Unit

Acknowledgements

With special thanks to Sadie Robarts, who helped put this pamphlet together; and to the NCCL Rights for Women Unit, Women against Rape, Edinburgh and Lothian Women's Aid and countless solicitors and barristers who contributed information.

Rights for Women Unit
National Council for Civil Liberties
21 Tabard Street, London SE1 4LA

Printed in Great Britain
by the Russell Press, Nottingham

Contents

The legal profession

It is only just over a century ago that a young woman called Sophia Jex-Blake went to court after she had been denied a place at Edinburgh University's medical school because of her sex. The bench of the Court of Sessions — 12 judges in all — deliberated as to whether women were, in common law, equal to men. By a majority, they found them not to be so. The notion of a woman as a 'legal person' — that is, of women's equality — was no match for the dogma of Victorian patriarchs.

This is just one historical example of how equality claims have foundered on the findings of eminent judges, then, as now, appointed as neutral and independent arbiters to uphold the law. But they also interpret the law, and thus reveal themselves as being not entirely 'without prejudice'.

This pamphlet will try to examine the ways in which the fabric of the law and the assumptions of an overwhelmingly male legal profession affect the lives of women who come into contact with it as lawyers, defendants, victims and complainants. It will look at the ways in which, despite the growing package of 'equal rights' won by women, the law and its servants, the judges, are plagued by stereotyped views of women.

The law, like most other professions, is dominated by men. They hold sway in all the areas, both inside and outside the courts, especially at the higher levels. A glance at the profession at work reveals an overwhelming male presence: judges, barristers, solicitors, clerks of the court, magistrates, court ushers, the police, defendants are all more likely to be men than women. There are just two areas where women do not play a minority role. There are the armies of secretaries who provide the back-up services, and, in recent years, women are well represented on juries.

The legal profession has been jealous of its own privileges while denying rights to others. Part of its reactionary platform has been to keep women out of its cosy and exclusive hierarchy. Towards the end of the 19th century, the legal establishment was stubbornly blocking women's advancement: it was fighting against votes for women, resisting women's entry into public life and, not surprisingly, denying women entry into its own ranks.

In the 1870s, an application by 92 women to attend lectures at Lincoln's Inn was turned down; it was 'not expedient' decreed the benchers, the senior members of the Inns of Court. Then again, in 1903, a group of women graduates, including Christabel Pankhurst, brought a test application requesting admission to the bar. This, too, was rejected. The legal elite fought their case on the grounds of professionalism — what they were arguing was that only men could maintain legal standards. In this way, maleness became obligatory. Alongside this was forged a style of behaviour and performance which defined the professional standards and thus reinforced the sort of male 'clubbiness' which still exists today.

Only from 1919, when the Sex Disqualification Removal Act opened the professions to women, were they allowed to train and practise as barristers and solicitors. Their progress has been slow and it is only in the past decade that their numbers have substantially increased. Even so, the percentage of practising women lawyers to men practitioners is lower than in other professions such as medicine or journalism. In 1982, out of 55,000 solicitors only 7621 (13.9 per cent) were women. Female barristers do marginally worse: out of a total of 4864 barristers, 582 (10.8 per cent) were women.

Almost all these women are concentrated on the lower rungs of the profession. At senior levels, there are pitifully few. There are three women High Court judges (the first woman was appointed in 1965) out of a total of 77, and 10 women circuit judges out of a total of 339. No woman has ever sat on the Judicial Committee of the House of Lords, the ultimate court of appeal.

The narrow recruitment base of British judges has not changed that much over the years. A typical profile of all those High Court judges appointed between 1980 and 1982 is of a 55-year-old white male, educated at one of the top public schools and Oxbridge and an experienced barrister and QC.

Although one-third of all law students are now women, far less than one-third become practising lawyers. There is discrimination against women training to be solicitors: they find it more difficult to secure jobs as articled clerks. And women barristers find even greater problems when they try to find a tenancy in a set of chambers, which is the sole way in which barristers can practise. In 1977, a Bow Group memorandum reporting to the Royal Commission on Legal Services said: 'Many chambers deliberately limit the number of women; and while female pupils are accepted the tenancies are consistently given to men.' There are still chambers with no women: this is legal for barristers; being self-employed, they are not covered by the Sex Discrimination Act.

Where women do find tenancies they tend to be channelled into specialist areas such as family law. It is difficult to know whether the low esteem of this specialism within the profession is because it is dominated by women or whether women are encouraged to practise in it because it is seen as women's work and a female area of expertise.

The facts then point to a well-entrenched, male-dominated profession where incursions by women are, in many cases, only grudgingly tolerated and then in the less prestigious and less well-paid jobs.

The male ethos in the profession is a more insidious expression of discrimination. The qualities of a good barrister tend to be associated with male arrogance, pomposity, 'erudition' and so on. Sadly, in the past, to achieve a measure of success women barristers were expected to ape this style conceived and exploited by men.

In court, traditional rituals can undermine female practitioners. Lawyers have to 'get on' with judges, not easy for women excluded as they are — even if only unconsciously from the male social network. There is a tendency to ignore women lawyers, to suggest their invisibility by using the collective 'gentlemen' when addressing counsel, even if it includes a woman. Judges may also invoke a sort of sexual or frivolous imagery which can unnerve women lawyers. One judge, seeing a group of women counsel waiting to go into court said: 'I see we've got the chorus girls here today.' Another judge, listening to a woman barrister making a vigorous argument, commented: 'I understand there's a special bridle used to restrain restless mares; I'm going to have to get one to restrain you.' Playing to the gallery, no doubt, but offensive and sexist to the barrister. The professionalism of women lawyers is questioned by the suggestion that they could manipulate a jury by their appearance. One woman barrister wearing her hair in a pony-tail rather than the required bun was called in to speak to the judge, who told her: 'Perhaps you would be at an advantage if you flicked your pony-tail at the men in the jury'.

And, as in other professions, opportunities for equality are threatened by those men with fossilised views on women's 'true purpose'. From *Not Without Prejudice*, the Memoirs of Sir David Napley (ex-President of the Law Society) comes this comment:

It is to their [female lawyers] benefit and that of their husbands and families that they have alternative interests to pursue when they have achieved what I consider to be their most important purpose in life, while possessing the means to sustain themselves if they are denied the opportunity to fulfil that main purpose.

Criminals

Women, by and large, are law-abiding. Far fewer women than men commit crimes, and the crimes they do commit are, in the main, minor ones. In 1980, men were found guilty of nearly two million offences while the number of offences for which women were found guilty totalled under 70,000.

Contrary to commonly held beliefs, women do not get off lightly in the courts. In 1975, five times as many adult females with no previous convictions were jailed than men with no previous convictions (*Probation Journal* 1977). In 1981, almost 4000 women were remanded in custody before their trial, but only one-third ended up with a prison sentence. Community service would appear to be an ideal punishment for women offenders (families, for example, for which women usually take responsibility, would be less likely to be broken up). In fact, male offenders are twice as likely as women to receive a community service order rather than a prison sentence.

Crime figures for women have risen fast in recent years. There were 1,120 women in prison in 1981 as against 35,549 men. For women, this represents a 65 per cent increase since 1970. Yet that was the year when the Home Office declared that 'as the end of the century draws nearer, penological progress will result in even fewer or no women at all being given prison sentences.' This golden age — so forcefully promised — is further off than ever.

Little attention is paid to women in prison: government studies remain unpublished and theories about their appropriate treatment are blurred and contradictory. They are treated, in fact, as an adjunct of the much larger male prison population while their own particular needs remain hidden and untreated.

The treatment that women receive as defendants in court depends to some extent on the images that men hold of women. Traditional assumptions focussed on women's passivity, weakness and piety. These qualities — coupled with a need for protection — were assumed to keep women within the law. Their assumed inferiority suggested a quality of childishness (see Judge Sutcliffe's comment, page 18); women, after all, were legal minors for many centuries. The woman who had stepped outside the law, thus defying her stereotype, was seen as an aberration — and for that aberration the woman had to be punished. The most fearsome response during the Middle Ages was the legal murder of thousands of women on charges of witchcraft.

Women's crimes tend to reflect their place in society: traditional women's crimes are linked to domestic life such as shop-lifting and social security fraud. But as women's role changes, so does women's crime. One woman barrister involved in criminal cases believes that judges sometimes feel affronted by women who have moved out of their traditional orbit of crime. Iris Mills, for example, who was one of the defendants in the anarchists' trial in 1979, said: 'I felt that the judge in my trial (Mr Justice King Hamilton who retired shortly after) couldn't understand me because I was a woman who hadn't been led astray by the men. The general impression you get is that everyone involved thinks women must be victims — you're either led astray or you're sick. If you're not that, you must be evil. I certainly felt that I was labelled as "bad". There was nothing that the judge actually did or said, it was just his general attitude and the way the whole system works which made me feel that.'

There is a sense in which women who commit crimes are treated sympathetically by the law. But this takes place within a framework of what judges see as 'normal' and 'respectable' behaviour. A sense of justice may not extend to women who, for whatever reasons, appear to have 'fallen from grace'. This clearly extends to one modern stereotype of the fallen woman, the prostitute, who is seen as having deliberately and knowingly rejected the 'decent' life. As such she may be treated more harshly by the courts.

One young woman who felt that she had no option but to turn to shoplifting and prostitution to support her child, suffered the harshest punishment — she lost the custody of her child.

Set against this image of the 'unworthy' mother is the view of women offenders as being sick rather than wilful. Men commit crimes for rational reasons; women because they are mentally unbalanced. The woman shoplifter, for one, neatly fits this description — she is seen as menopausal, unbalanced, rejected.

Then there are the cases of women who commit violent crime, 'domestic violence' stood on its head, when women attack men, often those who have subjected them to a lifetime of violence. There are no statistics which compare sentencing in crimes of violence against the opposite sex broken down by gender — these would clarify a controversial issue. Certainly, there are judges who look sympathetically at women defendants who have been 'driven to the end of their tether' by violent partners. However, these two examples reveal certain assumptions held by two judges in recent and well-publicised cases.

It is a very sad history. It is also a very sad duty I have to

perform because you deliberately and unlawfully stabbed
and killed your father . . . I bear in mind your suffering,
but the least sentences I can impose are three years in
prison for each of you.

Mr Justice Smith (*The Times*,
18 November 1980.)

What should be the attitude of the law to those who
unlawfully and with violence kill someone who has treated
them badly? . . . Can the law tolerate this kind of
behaviour when there are ample remedies?

Lord Justice Lawton at the Court of
Appeal (*The Times*, 4 December
1980.)

The Maw sisters, Annette and Charlene, had suffered years of violence from their drunken father. In court Mrs Maw, their mother, described how Mr Maw attacked Charlene: 'I pleaded with him to stop. I heard screaming and shouting. I went upstairs and saw him attacking Annette. Her forehead was bleeding and blood streaming down her face. I pushed him on the mattress and he screamed abusively. He said he was going to kill the girls. I have never been as frightened in my life.' The fight continued and Annette stabbed her father with a weapon passed to her by Charlene.

At the Court of Appeal, Annette Maw's three year sentence was upheld, but Charlene's was reduced from three years to six months.

There were various expedients open to a woman regularly
subjected to rough treatment by her husband, but a licence
to kill was not one of them . . . We cannot hold that the
sentence imposed was excessive — indeed it might well have
been higher.

From the Appeal heard in Edinburgh
against a six-year sentence given to
Mrs X for killing her violent
husband, November 1979. The appeal
was dismissed.

Mrs X had been subjected to the violence of her drunken husband for eight years when she stabbed him. 'I do remember that before it happened, after Jimmy had been arguing and shouting at me that he had that look in his eye that he always got before he assaulted me. He still had that Gurkha knife in the house and I was sure he was going to go for me with it.'

The story of Mrs X — of poverty, unemployment, bad accommodation (seven children and two adults in two bedrooms), the record of her drunken, drug-taking husband who had frequently been in prison, a suicide attempt — points up the futility of the judge's comments that there were various expedients open to her. A woman living under such conditions does not have options. One of the reasons why she stayed with her husband despite the quality of their life together was because of the children — once, when she did leave him two of her girls were taken into care.

The 'remedies' available to women who live their lives in the company of violent men were also referred to in the Maw sisters' trial — namely, the use of the Domestic Violence Act, the police and social services. But the police and social services are not always willing or able to intervene, and the use of the law is not, at least in the long term, always an effective way of protecting women. What judges fail to realise is the financial dependency of women on men, the practical impossibility in many cases of a woman finding alternative accommodation for herself and several children, or her ability to even make contact with a lawyer — a point unlikely to be perceived by a white, middle-class judge who finds the law so familiar and accessible.

Some were prostitutes, some were women of easy virtue, but the last six attacks involved victims whose reputations were totally unblemished.
Some were prostitutes, but perhaps the saddest part of the case is that some were not.
(She) drank too much, was noisy and sexually promiscuous.

The killings in the North of England by the Yorkshire Ripper created a monstrous climate of fear for women, particularly for those who lived in the area. Public reaction was outraged, especially when it was realised that all women — and not just prostitutes — were in danger. At the Ripper's trial, this division between 'good' and 'bad' women was futher reinforced by comments such as those above. But then prostitutes — but not their clients — have always been considered a 'separate' case.

Even today a woman can still be labelled a 'common' prostitute after being given two cautions for loitering or soliciting by a policeman (no witnesses are required). In court, the label 'common prostitute' can be read out as part of the evidence despite the fact that prostitution in itself is not a crime. Prostitution was decriminalised under the Street Offences Act, 1959, but, by the Act's objective 'to clear it off the streets', street walking was forbidden. Discrimination against women was written into the Act — soliciting was a crime whereas kerb-crawling by men on the look out for prostitutes was not although police action against kerb-crawlers has been implemented recently in some areas.

Women's groups are now calling for a change in the law. One important reform has already been implemented: from 31 January 1983 prostitutes could no longer be sent to prison. Some magistrates are finding a way round this by imposing huge fines and then imprisoning women for non-payment. Other reforms such as an end to the term 'common prostitute' and to soliciting and loitering as offences are still a campaign focus.

Domestic violence

Violence in the home is commonplace and nearly all the victims are women. Homicide, one might say, is a family affair. The largest single category of murders (24 per cent) are of spouse or cohabitant, and of these more than 80 per cent of the victims are women. In 1979, 163 women were murdered by a spouse or cohabitant as opposed to 37 men (Home Office figures).

The Home Office has only once — in 1979 — produced figures detailing violence between spouses. In the cases reported to the police — known to be only the tip of the iceberg — 91.5 per cent of cases involving wounding and serious assault were committed by the husband on his wife.

At all levels, the law does not appear to take domestic violence seriously. It is, in a sense, condoned by silence. Ignoring domestic violence is a legacy from the days when a woman was literally a man's property. Today, a woman may find her appeals ignored, to be told to go home and forget about it or even be herself blamed for male violence. One woman, subjected to her husband's violence, reported the attacks to the police. They took her into custody overnight and the next day she was released — into the 'care' of her husband.

The concept of the home as a private place and the family an incorruptible ideal with the man at its head still lingers on in the minds of the police, the courts and certain of our legislators.

This crime committed with a ligature so closely resembles the murder of your estranged wife that it may mean you are not just a domestic murderer, but a very dangerous man.

> Mr Justice Hodgson jailing Robert
> Finlay for life for rape while on bail
> awaiting trial for the murder of his
> wife, July 1982.

And again:

Before such assaults are said to inflict exceptional hardship, there must be something out of the ordinary in what happened.

> Lord Justice O'Connor at the Court
> of Appeal refusing a wife permission
> to divorce her violent husband within
> three years of marriage (*Spare Rib*,
> February 1982.)

The Domestic Violence Act 1976 provides an example of the ways in which the judiciary can, at least initially, hamper radical legislation. The Act, which was passed in a private member's bill after vigorous lobbying from women's groups, enables wives and cohabitees to be protected by the courts from violent men without the necessity of divorce proceedings. (In the past, women who were not married had no such protection if the man with whom they were living owned the home.)

When the first cases came before the county courts, there were judges who could not acknowledge that a law had been passed which gave priority to a woman's right to bodily security over a man's right over his property — the precious concept of an Englishman's home is his castle had at last been broken down. Appeals quickly went to the House of Lords who ruled that the law had indeed changed in this radical way.

Your conduct after what you did was extremely callous and I suspect calculated. But I have come to the conclusion that having spent 10 weeks in prison, and had the remorse which I am told you feel, you have suffered enough.

Mr Justice Mars-Jones sentencing Gordon Asher at Winchester Crown Court to six months imprisonment suspended for two years for the manslaughter of his wife (*The Times*, 9 June 1981.)

Jane Asher was killed in the bathroom of a house where she and her husband were attending a party. They had had a quarrel about Jane's relationships with other men. Gordon Asher held her by the throat and she suddenly collapsed on the floor. He carried her out of the house, drove six miles and buried her body at a roadworks' site.

The negligible sentence given to Asher is not representative of the punishment given to most killers. Why was his so lenient?

The attitudes of both the defence and the prosecution indicated that Jane Asher's character was somehow 'at fault'. She did not conform to the passive, faithful image of the 'good wife'. It was revealed in court that she had had lovers and that her behaviour at the party — dancing with other men — left much to be desired. Her description by the prosecution of Jane Asher as a 'two-timer', a 'flirt', a woman who 'made up to other men' was perhaps a cue for the dismissive attitude of the judge. The court seemed to be suggesting that her behaviour was somehow an 'excuse' for her violent death, and that she was responsible for her husband's violence.

One local woman who had campaigned against the Asher sentence said: 'The result of this case suggests a marriage licence is a licence to kill. Since the case, we have been told of men who have told their wives: "Look I can kill you and get away with it." '

Sadly, it was at Winchester Crown Court, one year later that another woman's killer was sent for trial. In this case, too, the victim did not escape the court's derision.

Mary Bristow with an IQ of 182 was a rebel from her middle-class background. She was unorthodox in her relationships, so proving that the cleverest people aren't always very wise. Those who engage in sexual relationships should realise that sex is one of the deepest and most powerful human emotions, and if you're playing with sex you're playing with fire. And it might be, members of the jury, that the conventions which surround sex, which some people think are 'old hat' are there to prevent people if possible from burning themselves.

From the summing up of Mr Justice Bristow, at Winchester Crown Court, June 1982, in the trial of Peter Wood. He was found not guilty of murder on the grounds of diminished responsibility but guilty of manslaughter and sentenced to six years imprisonment.

Mary Bristow died at her home in Winchester after being clubbed with a meat tenderiser, smothered and strangled. Her killer was a man who had once been her lover and for whom Mary felt sympathy, allowing him to stay in her house when he had nowhere to go. Wood insisted on intensifying their friendship and wanted to marry Mary. She turned him down.

Provocation was the main thrust of the defence at Wood's trial. 'Her rejection of him, perhaps in a rather nasty way,' said Wood's counsel Patrick Back QC, 'must have been like a stab in the body.'

Mary's refusal to have an exclusive sexual relationship with Wood was interpreted in court as a reasonable justification for Wood's action. No witnesses were allowed to speak out for Mary; Wood's description of her and what had happened were taken as fact. Her friends saw, as the trial unfolded, that it was Mary rather than Wood who was on trial. The character assassination was based on Mary's class, her intelligence, her politics, her views on marriage.

She was also middle-class, and as sometimes happens with very clever people she was in a state of rebellion against the morality favoured by that class. She regarded marriage as, at any rate, something not for her. I suppose she thought of it as something that would restrict her freedom. She was

a devotee of many causes. The Women's Liberation Movement, pro-abortion and CND demonstrations.
                              Patrick Back QC, defending Peter Wood.

Thus did Mary ask to be killed and was deemed responsible for her own death. Women's autonomy and demand for independence was a signal for the judiciary to undermine just such qualities.

The doctors agree and I am satisfied that the pressures were such as to make you mentally ill at the time so you weren't fully responsible for what you did. . . I believe that the order I propose to make is not simply merciful to you but right also to the community as a whole.
                              Mr Justice Mustill putting Douglas
                              Coles on probation for two years and
                              ordering him to receive in-patient
                              psychiatric treatment for the
                              manslaughter of his wife Ethel.
                       Leeds Crown Court, November 1980.

Douglas Coles hit his wife on the head with a glass paperweight. Ethel Coles was a hypochondriac: she made her husband take time off work to look after her and put pressure on him to sell their house and move. He had had a nervous breakdown.

The sympathetic attitude expressed by the judge in this case of a sad marriage which ended in violent death points up the contrast between the sentences imposed in this case and that of the Maw sisters (see page 10), sentenced only four days after this hearing, in the same court.

Rape

Rape is an emotive and specific example of male violence against women. The law on rape, the way it operates and the extent and limitations of the protection it offers women is not open to a gender comparison. Like against like cannot be compared. Men rape women. Women do not rape men.

The law defines rape as sexual intercourse without the woman's consent by force, fear or fraud. However, if a man honestly believes, no matter how unreasonable this belief might be, that the women consented, it is not rape.

There is no concept in law of rape inside marriage although a Private Member's Bill introduced in 1983 demanded reform. A married woman cannot bring a charge against her husband for rape unless a Decree of Judicial Separation has been granted by a court. However she may bring a charge of assault. Two hundred years ago, Judge Hale said:

> *The husband cannot be guilty of a rape committed by himself on his lawful wife for by their mutal matrimonial consent and contract the wife hath given herself in this kind unto her husband which she cannot retract.*

On this point, the law has not changed. When, in 1981, a man broke into his estranged wife's house and raped her, he was charged with assaulting her and fined £100, well below the maximum.

The heaviest sentence for rape is life. There is no minimum sentence. Thus judges have wide powers of discretion. Twenty-nine of the 420 men convicted of rape in England and Wales in 1980 did not get custodial sentences: 18 received suspended sentences, five were put on probation, three received community service orders, one was given a juvenile supervision order, another made subject of a care order and one was given a conditional discharge.

In recent years, the reactionary attitudes of judges while handing out light sentences to rapists has provoked considerable public anger. In Parliament, Jack Ashley MP has led a campaign for a mandatory prison sentence for rape. Commenting on the case of a rapist (that of Thomas Holdsworth, see page 20) who received a six month suspended sentence and was then set free by the Court of Appeal, he echoed the anger of women who see that by treating rapists leniently the rights of women are seriously undermined. He said 'If a judge, or member of the Royal Family, was ruptured, smashed to the ground and left there bleeding, I don't believe for one second that any member of the judiciary would give his assailant six months suspended sentence and then let him free. But because it was a woman, there's still the ancient belief that it somehow doesn't matter so much.'

One of the testing aspects of a rape trial is that there are usually no other witnesses. A jury must convict or acquit on the basis of the woman's evidence against the man. She is just the witness in the case in which she must prove her innocence. She has no counsel to represent her and no one to defend her. She is, in judicial terms, out there alone.

The corroboration warning is not required in law, but the judge invariably gives it to the jury. In some ways it reflects the courts' attitude that the women herself is on trial. Archbold, the practitioners' bible on criminal procedure, itself makes this point in its reference to the corroboration warning:

> *No particular formula is required but the jury should be warned in plain language that it is dangerous to convict on the evidence of the complainant alone, because experience has shown that female complainants have told false stories for various reasons, and sometimes for no reason at all. If a proper warning has been given the jury may convict on the complainant's uncorroborated evidence if they have no doubt that she is speaking the truth.*

> *It is well known that women in particular and small boys are liable to be untruthful and invent stories.*

Judge Sutcliffe, Old Bailey, April 1976.

Those who believe that rape victims lie might look to the report of the New York City Rape Analysis Squad which found that only two per cent of rape charges reported were false and that these figures were not out of step with false charges made for other serious crimes.

The Sexual Offences Act 1976 was designed to protect women from unnecessary interrogation into their previous sexual experiences. It was established that such evidence can only be introduced by an application made to the judge in the absence of the jury. However, in practice many applications are being allowed. In 60 per cent of rape trials applications are made, and out of these 75 per cent are allowed. (*New Law Journal*, August 1982).

The attitude of judges in their interpretation of this law is thus of vital importance. Judge Brian Gibbens, for one, is not impressed by the Act.

I think it might be unfair, perhaps even more so in an older woman, to prevent cross-examination on sexual proclivities, but that is what Parliament wants . . . This wretched section overturns many of our habits in criminal trials.

The Times, 10 February 1982.

So suspicion continues to fall on the victim as her lifestyle is called into question. As Zsuzanna Adler wrote in *The Times* (10 February 1982) after monitoring 50 Old Bailey rape cases in 1981: 'The relevance of such matters to the issue of consent is highly doubtful, but the general lifestyle of all but the most respectable victims was regularly scrutinised . . . As one lawyer said: "You have heard evidence about the sort of girl she is — you have to take that into account as a background to the case".'

It does not seem to me that the appellant is a criminal in the sense in which that word is used frequently in these courts. Clearly he is a man who, on the night in question, allowed his enthusiasm for sex to overcome his normal behaviour.

Mr Justice Slynn at the Court of
Appeal, June 1977.

The best thing you can do now to make amends is to go back to your unit and continue to serve your country.
Lord Justice Roskill presiding over
the same appeal case.

At the Court of Appeal, Guardsman Tom Holdsworth had his three-year sentence quashed. Instead, a six-month suspended prison sentence was substituted. Their Lordships agreed that Holdsworth was an asset to the British army and should be allowed to continue serving. (In the event he was thrown out of the army.) The implications of their decision was that it was Holdsworth's career which mattered and not his crime.

Holdsworth's 'enthusiasm for sex' involved an attack on a 17-year-old barmaid, whom he had met previously that evening, in a park. When the woman had refused to have sex, Holdsworth kept on touching her, pulled at her clothes, and put his hand up her vagina (he was wearing rings), not just once but several times. On one occasion she had passed out with the pain. He also grabbed her round the ribs, bit her nipples and wrenched her earrings out. The doctor who examined her said that the extreme swelling of the vulva would have caused extreme pain which he had only seen in cases of recent childbirth. Again the injury was not consistent with normal intercourse and a great deal of force would have been necessary.

Faced with these facts, Mr Justice Slynn said:

As it was said by Lord Justice Roskill during the course of the argument, it is probable that this girl would have been less severely injured if in fact she had submitted to rape by the mere threat of force rather than force being applied in the way it was.

But this sort of argument puts women in a double bind — in which either way they are the losers. If they 'submit to rape' they can well be accused of not resisting fiercely enough (see the comments of Judge Wild below); if they do resist — as in the Holdsworth case — they run the risk of terrible injury, or even death.

Women who say no do not always mean no. It is not just a question of saying no, it is a question of how she says it, how she shows and makes it clear. If she doesn't want it she only has to keep her legs shut and she would not get it without force and there would be marks of force being used.

> Judge David Wild at Cambridge
> Crown Court, 1982, summing up in a
> case in which a man was acquitted of
> rape.

The woman had met the man in a pub and then went with him to a basement flat. She had claimed that she had submitted to rape because she was frightened of being injured. She had, she said, put up a struggle and made it clear that she did not want sex. She had not screamed because she lost her voice when she was frightened.

Judge Wild's comments carried a host of ill-judged assumptions about women. He raised the old adage that women don't mean it when they say 'no' — that assumes that women are irrational and quixotic, do not know their own minds and automatically indulge in sexual games play. He also accepted there must be extensive injury to the woman before rape is likely. Yet it is unacceptable to base consent on the lack of a victim's injuries — how real is consent if there's a knife at your throat? It is perfectly proper for a woman to claim it was not consent if she were raped for fear of being hurt or killed.

I am not saying that a girl hitching home late at night should not be protected by the law, but she was guilty of a great deal of contributory negligence.

> Judge Bertrand Richards sitting at
> Ipswich Crown Court, 1982, during a
> rape case in which he fined a man
> £2000 for raping a 17-year-old
> woman.

Judge Richards' comments were endorsed by Sir Melford Stevenson, the retired 81-year-old High Court judge who said: *'It is the height of impudence for any girl to hitch-hike at night. That is plain, it isn't really worth stating. She is in the true sense asking for it.'*

The court heard that the young woman had been visiting her fiancé at an American base where he was a serviceman. When he discovered that, at the last moment, he was unable to drive her home she had no option but to hitch a lift — there was no public transport, she was forbidden to stay the night at the base and she had promised her parents she would be home by midnight. The man who gave her a lift drove her to Thetford Forest and raped her.

The first point to make is a legal one: 'contributory negligence' has no validity in the law of rape. As Sir Michael Havers, the Attorney General, said later: 'Contributory negligence is a legal concept relevant only in actions for damages in civil courts.' Judge Richards' source of information was an outdated edition of a standard text book on sentencing; the current edition, however, is only a marginal improvement and still makes the point of 'imprudent behaviour'.

Provoking or encouraging a man is often one of the main platforms of the defence's argument in rape cases. Hitch-hiking comes in this category. The suggestion is made that a woman who hitch-hikes is not 'sensible'. In this instance the woman had no choice — no other means of getting home. But whether she is sensible or not dodges the issue that rape must be seen as a serious offence under any circumstances. The outcry which followed Judge Richards' remarks focussed on the concept that a woman hitch-hiking was unlikely to find redress from the law and that any man who gave a lift to a woman could rape her with little fear of punishment. These remarks caused outrage in circles beyond activists in the women's movement, thus forcing into the public arena new debate about men's violence towards women.

Family law

The stirrings in the 17th century of the notion of a rational society in which the individual had protection under the law did not extend to women. As Mary Astell, in 1700, cried, in exasperation: 'If all Men are born free, how is it that all Women are born slaves?' It was a fair question. In law, women were 'under couverture'. They were seen as legal minors. When a woman married, whatever she owned became her husband's. She herself could be disposed of, how and when her husband wished: women could even be put up for sale in the most humiliating circumstances. If a woman left her husband, he could refuse maintenance and demand the right to any money she might have earned to support herself. And anyone giving refuge to a runaway wife could be sued by the husband for loss of services.

It was not until the middle of the 19th century that a husband who neglected to maintain his wife — for this was his obligation in the marriage contract — could be brought before the magistrates court. But this had to be initiated by the parish guardian or overseer — no wife could do it on her own behalf.

As society firmed up its belief in the privacy of the home the man as the head of the household became the entrenched ideal. And as the wife was his 'property' so were his children. The father's 'rights' over his children were natural; thus paternal custody, too, was natural.

The swing towards mothers' rights and concern for the welfare of the children began with the Custody of Infants Act of 1839, which said that in certain circumstances fathers did not have the absolute right of ownership. For example, mothers were allowed to keep children under seven years old and have access to older children provided they had not committed the matrimonial offence of adultery. The rights of mothers to apply for custody were further extended in 1873, but there was no concept of equal guardianship until 1925 when mothers gained the same rights as fathers to apply to the courts for custody of their children.

This was implemented by the Guardianship of Infants Act 1925 which consolidated the growing concern for children which had first been recognised nearly a century earlier. The principle now was that in deciding custody disputes the welfare of the child should be paramount. And since the importance of the maternal role was now recognised, women's chances of gaining custody of their children improved by leaps and bounds. The thinking behind this, though, was more pro-child than pro-woman.

Over and above all this was the contentious issue of a woman's morality and her 'fitness' to be a mother.

It could never be in the interests of the child to be entrusted to the care of a woman who had committed adultery.

Judge Wallington, 1950, justifying his decision to award the care and control of a two-year-old girl to her father.

Nowadays, there is an attempt to distinguish the two roles of wife and mother, although a father may well retain *legal* custody over the children while giving a mother the day-to-day care and control if her behaviour is considered questionable by the courts. And the judiciary would take a more critical view of a woman who left her husband and children than of a man who abandoned his wife and children.

A woman's role is seen as being with her children; it is to her credit to be with them, to reinforce the notion of woman as mother figure. It would appear that the judiciary has little time for a more equal approach to parenting.

'A man ought not to give up work and turn himself into a mother figure or nanny at the expense of the state,' said Mr Justice Payne in a divorce case involving a man who had given up his job to look after his baby girl. *'Such a role is not primarily a male province . . . his brain should be used in work.'*

Spare Rib, July 1979.

Alternative life-styles, political activities, involvement in the women's movement have all been taken into account by judges as a feature of a woman's worthiness to gain custody of her child. Often they are used against her. But most controversial of all is the issue of lesbian mothers. The first lesbian to gain custody of her children won her case at the Appeal Court in 1976. The judges gave June Whitfield the custody of her 11-year-old twins but stressed that their decision was based on concern for the welfare of the children (the father could not provide suitable accommodation) rather than the question of the mother's lesbianism. 'I hope that no one will regard this as containing my judgement for or against homosexual parents,' said Lord Justice Ormrod.

This was a considerable victory. But, in general, lesbian mothers do not find they are given a sympathetic hearing in the courts. Judges are faced with not just a denial of the nuclear family but a rejection of the heterosexual family.

The most recent legislation in family law has been the Matrimonial Causes Act 1973 which perhaps represents the highpoint of legislation in favour of women. This Act entitles women to claim a share of the assets of the household and maintenance for herself and her children. The judiciary were enjoined on the breakdown of marriage to ensure that the wife's financial position remained the same as if the marriage had continued. But because many men now move into a new relationship with new family responsibilities the impossibility of getting 'a quart out of a pint pot' as one judge put it, causes grievances to all parties.

The Act also included a reference to the conduct of the parties in a divorce case. The court 'must exercise its powers so as to place the parties as far as it is practicable and having regard to their conduct, just to do so' in the financial position they would have been in if the marriage had not broken down.

The case of Watchel v. Watchel in 1973 gave an indication of how judges would interpret the Act. As a starting-point, one-third of the joint resources were to go to the wife. This would only be reduced if there had been 'gross and obvious' conduct said Lord Denning. In the same case, Mr Justice Ormrod said:

'Conduct subsequent to the separation by either spouse may affect the discretion of the court in many ways, e.g. the appearance of signs of financial recklessness in the husband or of some form of socially unacceptable behaviour by the wife which would suggest to a reasonable person that in justice modification to the order ought to be made.'

The concept of 'gross and obvious' may be used in cases involving violence. In Jones v. Jones, for example, the husband attacked the wife so she could never work again. The court's decision was that their house should be transferred to her. Again, in Armstrong v. Armstrong, the wife had shot the husband in the hand; consequently her share was cut from one-third to one-quarter. But by and large the concept of blame had disappeared until the Law Commission's discussion paper *The Financial Consequences of Divorce* in 1980 recommended that a partner's behaviour should be taken into account when it would be 'inequitable' to disregard it. This was taken up by the Matrimonial and Family Proceedings Bill of 1983. Those lobbying for reform believed that the decisions of the courts had swung too far in favour of women. The Bill also incorporates a cut-off point after which some wives would receive no more maintenance. Yet there is little evidence to support the idea that many ex-wives get a meal ticket for life and live off the fat of the land. And subjective decisions as to what constitutes grounds for a reduction in maintenance could work against women faced with a judge with little understanding of or sympathy for women's lives.

Since the divorce reforms of the 1970s there has been progress in formally recognising a woman's domestic labour as a contribution to the family assets. But before that, Lord Denning could argue:

> *'The wife does not get a share in the house simply because*
> *she cleans the walls or works in the garden or helps her*
> *husband with the painting or decorating. Those are the sort*
> *of things which a wife does for the benefit of a family*
> *without altering the title to, or interest in, the property.'*
> (*Button* v. *Button*, 1968).

The notorious cases in the United States of claims for 'palimony' have publicised the notion of 'mistresses' rights'. As wives have earned recognition to be compensated for making an economic contribution to the home, so have mistresses gained some recognition from the courts of their input into the joint home. Although a mistress has no right or obligation to be maintained by her ex-partner, she may be entitled to some money if it is seen that she made a contribution to the house. The financial dependency of the woman is highlighted in this relationship: a man claiming money from a woman with whom he has lived would most probably be found feckless and undeserving.

This attitude is at the crux of the problem: husbands are seen as the providers and women as being economically dependent on them. There are no grounds for a 'meal ticket for life' for wives but until there are more opportunities for women to be economically independent, it is vital for both husbands and wives that a just system of maintenance is developed.

Civil rights

Enormous progress has been made towards women's full citizenship and their right to be treated as legal 'persons' in every aspect of life. But there are still important pockets of the law which discriminate against women. Our immigration law, for example, is both racist and sexist. All men are allowed — in theory, if not in practice — to bring their wives and fiancées into this country; the same right is not, however, extended to women who were not themselves born in this country nor had parents who were born here. Effectively, this precludes non-white women from enjoying such a basic right. Again, the British Nationality Act of 1981 has removed the right of a foreign wife to acquire citizenship upon her marriage although she may apply for naturalisation.

Our social security and taxation laws also throw up elements of discrimination based on the traditional notion that the man is the breadwinner, the woman the dependant. Some changes in the social security legislation are, however, imminent, forced on the government by an EEC directive. In November 1983 family income supplement became available to whichever parent in a two-parent family is in work, and at the same time married or cohabitating women could, in certain circumstances, be nominated the 'breadwinner' and were able to claim Supplementary Benefit, until then a right only available to men. In the taxation system women are generally assessed as financial appendages of their husbands. The Conservative administration of 1979-83 published a Green Paper which discussed different ways of amending the present law. While reform was mentioned in the Conservative 1983 election manifesto, the Government has not yet publicly announced their preferred option. However, it is feared that husband and wife will still be viewed as a unit and some form of transferable allowance for non-employed wives adopted.

The principle of equal rights for men and women has been law for less than a decade. The two Acts which enshrine this concept are the Equal Pay Act of 1970, which came into force in 1975, and the Sex Discrimination Act of 1975.

Despite the Equal Pay Act, women's average hourly earnings are still less than 75 per cent of men's and the Equal Opportunities Commission believes that there is unlikely to be any significant improvement 'as long as the law remains unaltered'. This opinion is reflected by the numbers of women seeking redress under the Equal Pay Act: 1742 applications were made in 1976 but by 1982 the numbers had dropped to 39. It is now clear that women can not look to the law with any confidence to remedy inequalities in their earnings. Our law has already been criticised by the European Court of Justice for ignoring European law on equal pay.

The Sex Discrimination Act makes it unlawful to treat a woman less favourably that it would treat a man in the same circumstances just because she is a woman. It covers education, training, employment, housing and the provision to the public of goods, services and facilities. It does not, though, embrace social security, taxation or the State pension age. A person must also not be treated differently in employment because of their marital status. The Act covers not just direct discrimination, but also 'indirect' discrimination: this means that it is discriminatory to impose a condition which is more easily met by more people of one sex than the other.

The law itself, though, is a minefield of problems and very difficult to understand. Even when an applicant believes she has a good case, it is up to her to prove it — the burden of proof is on her to prove discrimination.

Cases under the Equal Pay Act and employment cases under the Sex Discrimination Act are heard in industrial tribunals where the chairperson is a lawyer sitting with two lay-persons, one from each side of industry. Most of those who sit in judgement on tribunals are, not surprisingly, men although there should be a woman on tribunals hearing discrimination cases. On appeal, cases are sent to the Employment Appeal Tribunal and can from there be referred to the Court of Appeal.

Only a minority of complainants are successful. In 1982 out of 39 applications under the Equal Pay Act only two were upheld and out of 150 cases under the Sex Discrimination Act only 17 cases received compensation. Many of the cases never reach the tribunal — they are either withdrawn or there is a conciliated settlement out of court. But there is some evidence to suggest that women are being dissuaded from pursuing their case by the Advisory, Conciliation and Arbitration Service once they have made an application.

Women who have taken their cases to an industrial tribunal come up against not just the complexity of interpreting the law but also against sexism. That this should be perpetuated within the judiciary in the interpretation of the Acts comes as no surprise to practitioners within this area of the law. Most judges and tribunal adjudicators who hear sex discrimination cases are notoriously uninformed and unsympathetic to what can constitute discrimination within the spirit of the legislation.

Lawyers representing complainants in discrimination cases, in order to prove their case, have had to educate the judiciary in the most basic premises of sex discrimination, and have often met serious resistance and hostility to these concepts which are embodied in the legislation.

It would be very wrong, to my mind, if the statute were thought to obliterate the differences between men and women or to do away with chivalry and courtesy which we expect mankind to give to womankind.

The words of Lord Denning, then Master of the Rolls, in the Court of Appeal *(Peake* v. *Automotive Products Ltd)* were quoted by Judge Ruttle in his judgement at Westminster City Court on 26 May 1978 on the application by Sheila Gray, a photographer, against El Vino Co Ltd (a wine bar in London's Fleet Street) alleging discrimination under the Sex Discrimination Act of 1975. Sheila Gray lost. So did Tess Gill, a lawyer, and Anna Coote, a journalist, who in February 1981 brought another action against El Vino's.

What all three women were demanding was the right to stand at the bar of El Vino's as male customers did, rather than abide by a long-standing rule which required women to sit at a table and be served there by a waitress. They argued that they were being less favourably treated than a man. Ms Britton, a witness for Ms Gray, found the rule embarrassing. She was 'mortified to be banished to a table and to be refused the same treatment as my professional equals.' Ms Coote found the rules extremely offensive. She felt singled out as being unequal to men and said that it was a demeaning experience to have to sit in the smoking room.

The management of El Vino's claimed that their rule was advantageous to women; it was explained that the bar was small, the wine racks were near floor level and the rule 'spared women the discomfort and indignity of being pushed and jostled by the men in the bar as well as being spared the embarrassment which could be caused when the male staff were removing bottles from the wine rack near floor level.'

Judge Ruttle agreed with the manager:

> *'I accept his evidence that the policy operated by his company was in no way designed to be adverse or hostile to women but, on the contrary, was aimed at promoting and preserving their dignity, respect and comfort.'*

The concepts of chivalry and courtesy have long been used to operate against women. In the 19th century the idea of male 'protectiveness' was used to stop women gaining the vote, to stop them getting jobs (except, of course, menial ones) and taking part in public life. It trapped them by 'putting them on a pedestal'; it curtailed their freedom by protecting them from so-called hardships.

In the last half of the 20th century, two judges came to the same conclusion in this case.

Judge Ranking, giving judgement in the Gill and Coote application, in 1982, also quoted the manager, Mr Bracken, who claimed that his male customers liked the rule: 'They think it unladylike to stand at the bar.' The nature of femininity and the 'natural' and desirable behaviour of women was also under scrutiny. At one point, the manager said they did not want 'the boiler suit brigade'.

Judge Ranking declared that the criteria of 'chivalry and sensible administrative arrangements' were not of particular significance; the case turned simply on 'whether ladies are less favourably treated than men'. In his view, the plaintiffs' reaction to the 'house rule' at El Vino's was 'somewhat extreme compared to what I would consider to be the reaction of the reasonable person.' They were clearly not 'reasonable' for Judge Ruttle, like Judge Ranking before him had decided that women were not unfavourably treated. The fact that they, unlike the male customers, had no choice as to where they could drink was not, so these county court judges deemed, discriminatory. Fortunately, the Court of Appeal did.

> *I must acknowledge at the outset that it appears to me to be trivial and banal even when topped up with much legalistic froth.*
>
> *In the light of the history those claims [of discrimination] are in my view, artificial and pretentious; but the industrial tribunal thought otherwise and their only*

*concern appear to have been as to how great a sum they
could award to this excessively outraged victim of sex
discrimination.*

Lord Justice Shaw sitting at the
Court of Appeal, 24 July 1981

Rosalind Coleman had been dismissed from her job as a travel
agent the day after her marriage because her husband worked for a
rival firm and the two employers, worried by the possibility of leaks
between husband and wife, had sacked the wife.

An industrial tribunal decided for Mrs Coleman on the grounds
that the employer's assumptions that the husband was the
breadwinner of the family constituted discrimination under the
SDA. The industrial tribunal awarded her £1666 compensation
including £1000 for injury to her feelings. On appeal, the
Employment Appeal Tribunal judged that there was no
discrimination. Mr Justice Slynn said:

*'It seems to us here that there really was no material upon
which the tribunal could conclude that this employer
treated Mrs Coleman less favourably than he treated or
would have treated a man employed by him in the same
situation.'*

There was no evidence, said the EAT, to suggest what would
have happened if Mrs Coleman had been the so-called
breadwinner. The EAT thought the husband would then have been
dismissed. Thus there was no material to suggest discrimination.
But the EAT had made no effort to define 'breadwinner', nor was
it viewed as discriminatory to assume Mr Coleman was the
breadwinner. Yet this assumption is one of the most blatant and
offensive expressions of sexism.

At the Court of Appeal, Mrs Coleman won (no thanks to Lord
Justice Shaw who dissented). Her award though for injury to
feelings was reduced to £100 (Lord Justice Shaw would have
reduced it even further to 'a thousand pence'). The EOC called it a
'significant' decision to establish that the assumption that Mr
Coleman was the breadwinner meant that Mrs Coleman had been
treated less favourably than if she had been a man. So general
assumptions about women, based on conventional stereotyping can
amount to unlawful discrimination — even if it takes an appeal to
the top of the judicial ladder to establish it.

This is a rule [(i.e. not employing women with young children] which the respondent reasonably applies as a matter of business necessity, and we therefore find that he has met the requirement to justify the use of a condition applied to employment . . .

From part of the judgement heard at
the industrial tribunal, 1980, in the
case of *Hurley* v. *Mustoe*.

Ursula Hurley, married with four children, was employed as a waitress at a London bistro, but after her first evening's work the owner, Mr Mustoe, arrived and she was then told that it was his policy not to employ women with young children and that she would have to go. The owner found such women unreliable. Ms Hurley took her case to an industrial tribunal where she lost.

Extraordinarily, the tribunal accepted the owner's policy not to employ *anyone* who had small children. But he had advertised for 'waitresses' and there was no evidence to suggest that he refused to employ men with dependent children. It was women with small children which he objected to.

The tribunal also found that it was justifiable for Mr Mustoe to make his 'no women with small children' requirement because it was necessary for his business. But as the Employment Appeal Tribunal later pointed out: 'Even if, for this purpose only, one concedes that *some* women with small children are less reliable than those without, it does not follow that it is necessary in order to achieve reliability to exclude *all* women with children.'

The EAT found for Ms Hurley and she was instructed to return to the industrial tribunal to be assessed for financial compensation: the industrial tribunal awarded her 50p for injury to feelings and £160 compensation. Their argument partly focussed on an issue outside the immediate one. Demonstrations held outside the bistro, supporting a woman's right to work, were seen to have had a 'remedial' effect on the applicant's feelings since she had attended one of them. It was also stated that her past experience as a waitress at Dingwall's Dance Hall would have given her 'experience in the adversities of life'. This, too, was used against her.

Throughout, the industrial tribunal clearly refused to see anything discriminatory in the way Ms Hurley was treated. Indeed, they were reluctant to see the need for her to go out to work at all despite the fact that more than half of all women with dependent children work and make an often vital contribution to the family income. 'The tribunal takes the view that, with family allowances, it might not have been essential, and it would depend upon the standard of living sought by the married couple.' Back to the home was the prescription the tribunal would dearly have enjoyed enforcing.

An appeal against the compensation awarded for injury to feelings was successful and Ms Hurley was finally awarded £100.

She was not dismissed on the assumed fact because she was a woman; she was dismissed on those facts because she was pregnant. It was only an accident of nature that pregnancy was restricted to the female sex.

Part of the judgement of the
industrial tribunal in the case of
Turley v. *Allders Department Stores*,
1979.

In order to see if she has been treated less favourably than a man the sense of the section is that you must compare like with like, and you cannot. When she is pregnant a woman is no longer just a woman. She is a woman, as the Authorised Version accurately puts it, with child, and there is no masculine equivalent.

Mr Justice Bristow at the
Employment Appeal Tribunal in the
same case, November 1979.

Kim Turley claimed that she was dismissed by her employers because she was pregnant. Her employer claimed she was sacked for bad time-keeping and poor performance. She had not worked long enough for protection from 'unfair dismissal' on the grounds of pregnancy under the Employment Protection Act. Instead she brought her complaint under the Sex Discrimination Act. At the industrial tribunal she lost, and then again, by a majority decision at the EAT. The dissenting voice sensibly argued that pregnancy is a medical condition which might require time off work in the same way that a sick man might need time off. The employer, she said, 'must not discriminate by applying different and less favourable criteria to the pregnant woman than to the man requiring time off. That is the like for like comparison not one between women who are pregnant and men who cannot become pregnant.'

Most women still work in traditional 'women's jobs' and despite the Sex Discrimination Act there remains protective legislation which defines certain jobs which women still cannot do — mining is the best-known example. But there are women who are moving into traditional 'men's jobs' like plumbing and carpentry.

The following examples show how women who had tried to break into the manual trades fared at two industrial tribunals.

Janet Krengel worked on a building site as a labourer for two months in 1976. In an argument over her pay packet, she swore at her boss and was dismissed. She took her case of unfair dismissal under the Sex Discrimination Act to an industrial tribunal. The issue was, as her counsel put it, whether a man would have been dismissed in the same circumstances and for the same reasons as was Mrs Krengel.

The majority sitting on the tribunal found against her. Once again, the dissenting voice was a woman, who drew from the evidence her conclusion that no other employee who had been dismissed was so treated because of swearing; there was always another reason. And in two cases, male employees who had sworn at the boss had not been dismissed and were still working for him.

We have tried to listen to the experiences of other women on other courses and their general complaints as to how individuals . . . reacted to the glances of men at her figure which cannot have anything possibly to do with discrimination against her, still less with discrimination against the applicant . . . We became more doubtful as to whether she was so keenly motivated as she alleges and felt more that she may well have merely regarded her application for the course as being an interesting new experience.

From the decision of the industrial tribunal in which Helen Sanders' application of discrimination was dismissed unanimously, June 1979.

Helen Sanders was dismissed from a TOPS carpentry course in Leeds after the three-week training period. She alleged that her work was of a high enough standard to continue and would have been higher if she had not encountered hostility from members of staff. Her attempt to describe her sense of isolation as the only woman on the course and the way her confidence was undermined was heard unsympathetically.

Ms Sanders' counsel also attempted to explain to the tribunal that her client had suffered indirect discrimination because of educational disadvantage and that provisions to remedy this — that is, positive action — are embodied in the Sex Discrimination Act. But the response was that such suggestions were impractical. Indeed they came round to the view that previous training might be a disadvantage since 'bad habits may have to be unlearned'. Yet they had stated that Ms Sanders' history was not 'the kind from which one could conclude that she must have been by her nature a potential carpenter or joiner.'

Subsequently Helen Sanders enrolled on another TOPS carpentry course and passed with flying colours.

Recommendations

There is no reason why British legislation (except that which is itself discriminatory) need have an adverse impact on women. However, our laws are administered by predominantly white, middle-class, middle-aged males who, in their professional lives, often express stereotype notions about women and show little understanding of the nature of women's lives. To counteract this situation, we feel that specific training is vital.

Training on the impact of the legal system on women should be compulsory for all those who administer the law. This includes judges, magistrates, members of tribunals, police, prosecuting lawyers and court officials.

Law students should also be given some form of training along the same lines, whether they are going to be barristers or solicitors.

In cases where women's issues are raised, consideration should be given to the appointment of lay assessors to sit with the judge or chair. In cases such as are referred to in this pamphlet we think this should be someone with special training or expertise in women's issues, and preferably a woman. It is already the practice to have at least one adjudicator who is a woman when sex discrimination cases are heard in the Industrial Tribunal.

Training for judges

In France and Italy judges undergo specific training to qualify as judges. They are career judges, unlike the British judges who are appointed from among senior barristers. We believe that the British system is prejudicial to women. One effect of the French and Italian training system is that it produces more women judges. In France, for example, 30 per cent of judges are women and, among current students training to be judges, 50 per cent are women.

1. Special training should be given to judges and those who chair Industrial Tribunals to educate them about the intent of legislation, such as the Sex Discrimination Act, Equal Pay Act and Domestic Violence Act, passed specifically to help women.

2. Judges' training should help judges become aware of stereotyped attitudes to women. This should be for all judges, whether they sit in civil or criminal courts. It is not so long since, in personal injuries cases, aging judges peered in the well of the court to assess a widow's likely prospect of remarriage in deciding how much to award her for the loss of her breadwinner husband.

Criminal law

1. Criminal judges should have regular training in the principles of sentencing. We do not advocate that imprisonment is necessarily the most satisfactory way of dealing with crimes against women, but it is one of the few ways there is of registering society's disapproval of such crimes. There should be no disparity in sentencing based on sex for similar offences. Sexist attitudes should not result in women getting heavier sentences than men for what are regarded as 'domestic' assaults or crimes of passion. Statistics should be kept so that comparisons can be made between the sentences given to men and women for the same offences.

In sentencing, the interests of children should be taken into account when imprisonment is being considered, particularly if the individual concerned has childcare responsibilities.

2. Guidelines with the same force as the Judges Rules should be issued so that prosecuting barristers are aware of the need to safeguard the interests of women victims of violent or sexual crimes.

3. In cases such as rape, the defence often relies on sexist stereotypes of women, thus it is important for the prosecutor to have had some special training so that she/he can protect the interest and reputation of the woman victim. The prosecutor should also have the duty to do this.

If prosecutors are not to be given this responsibility, then women victims of violent crime who have to give evidence should be entitled to be legally represented so that any attack on their character which relies on sexist stereotypes may be refuted. This is particularly important where the proceedings concern a woman who has been murdered, since her family have no redress in the form of defamation proceedings.

Alternatively, a legal counsel should act as a 'watching brief' appointed by family or friends of the victim to defend her reputation.

4. Prostitutes who solicit for clients on the street are charged with an offence. Kerbcrawlers, their prospective clients, are, in the main, not. In the light of this discrepancy we would recommend amendments on the laws about soliciting.

Rape

1. Rape in marriage should be illegal. The law should not allow a man to have sexual intercourse with a woman, by force and without her consent, simply because he is married to her.

2. The legal definition of rape should be extended to include

other forms of serious sexual assault involving penetration of the vagina or anus or oral-genital contact.

3. The rules of evidence should be amended so that details of a woman's personal life which are unconnected to her relationship with her attacker should be regarded as inadmissible. The Sexual Offences Act should be tightened up. Judges' directions to the jury should make it absolutely clear that absence of injury and signs of struggle do not amount to evidence of a woman's consent.

4. A more rational sentencing policy is needed, but we are opposed to mandatory sentencing for rape. In rape as in other criminal cases, sentencing should aim at rehabilitation and protecting the community, not at punishment for its own sake.

5. Many women are discouraged from reporting rape for fear of police procedure. We recommend that procedure is changed along the lines proposed by the Rape Counselling and Research Project in their evidence to the Royal Commission on Criminal Procedure (see *The Rape Controversy* by Melissa Benn, Anna Coote and Tess Gill, NCCL).

6. There should be a proper after-care service for rape victims run by social service departments and the NHS. The work of Rape Crisis Centres should be extended.

Family law

1. Civil judges dealing with custody and adoption should receive some specific training, backed with statistical information, to show that the traditional nuclear family is no longer necessarily the only model of family life and that alternative living arrangements — single mothers or fathers, communal households, lesbian couples — could be acceptable provided the quality of childcare is good.

2. We feel that Family Courts, with a conciliation rather than adversarial approach, should be introduced in line with the proposals of the Finer Report. Individuals with relevant expertise appointed by both the court and the parties concerned should sit with the judge so that a decision is reached in the best interest of the children rather than on the basis of lawyers scoring points.

The court itself should be as informal and unintimidating as possible and should be planned in a round-table fashion rather than the judge sitting at one end on a raised platform.

3. In injunction proceedings under the Domestic Violence Act, each case should be heard by one judge from beginning to end. Different judges hearing the same case at different stages can lead to delays and contradictions stemming from the differing attitudes of the judges.

Childcare

The childcare allowance for parents who are jurors should be more widely publicised so that those entitled apply for it. There should be facilities at courts dealing with family cases for children to be looked after and for nursing mothers to feed their children.

Sex Discrimination cases

1. Substantial consolidation and amendment of the equality laws is urgently required (see *Amending the Equality Laws* by Catherine Scorer and Ann Sedley, NCCL).

2. The regulations should be amended so that applicants in Sex Discrimination and Equal Pay cases can be legally aided.

3. Special training should be given to ACAS officials who attempt to mediate in equality claims.